MEDITATIONS
OF
WALT
WHITMAN

Earth,
My Likeness

T0160819

Compiled and edited by
CHRIS HIGHLAND

WILDERNESS PRESS

Meditations of Walt Whitman: Earth, My Likeness

1st EDITION October 2004

Front cover portrait by Mathew Brady.
    Courtesy Walt Whitman Collection, Clifton Waller Barrett
    Library, University of Virginia
Other cover photos copyright © 2004 by Chris Highland
Interior photos, except where noted, by Chris Highland
Frontispiece portrait courtesy Bayley-Whitman Collection,
    Ohio Wesleyan University
Book and cover design by Larry B. Van Dyke

ISBN 978-0-89997-362-3

Manufactured in the United States of America

Published by: **Wilderness Press**
              c/o Keen Communications
              P.O. Box 43673
              Birmingham, AL 35243
              (800) 443-7227; FAX (205) 326-1012
              info@wildernesspress.com
              www.wildernesspress.com

Visit our website for a complete listing of our books and for
ordering information.

Cover photos: Walt Whitman (ca. 1862); Maples in Spring—
                  Samuel P. Taylor State Park, California;
                  Forget-Me-Nots in Brick—San Geronimo Valley,
                  California; Water Lily—Conservatory of
                  Flowers, Golden Gate Park, San Francisco,
                  California
Frontispiece: Walt Whitman (ca. 1854)

MEDITATIONS
OF
WALT
WHITMAN

Earth,
My Likeness

To Carol
"there in that tree"

Contents

"Thou knowest the prayers and vigils of my youth,
Thou knowest my manhood's solemn and visionary
    meditations,
Thou knowest how before I commenced I devoted all to
    come to Thee,
Thou knowest I have in age ratified all those vows and
    strictly kept them,
Thou knowest I have not once lost nor faith nor ecstasy
    in Thee..."

~ Walt Whitman
from *"Prayer of Columbus"*

Introduction

"Afoot and light-hearted I take to the open road,
Healthy, free, the world before me,
The long brown path before me
leading wherever I choose..." [1]

With these buoyant, libertarian words, Walt
Whitman (1819–1892), the consummate
American poet of the earth, invites us along on his
journey universal. He is, for us, the vagabond voyager of the soul. Or, to mix and shake the metaphor,
he is the seasoned salt of the earth, sprinkling himself over the landscape and giving our steps a savory
taste.

Walt Whitman traveled across the continent,
soaking the ink of the wilds and the urban into his
pen. His long brown path stretched out from his
home in Long Island, New York, to Brooklyn, New
Orleans, Chicago, Washington and New Jersey.
Working variously as a printer, journalist, teacher
and Civil War nurse, Whitman deeply felt the pulse
of his native land, and came away with dark blood
on his hands and a light song on his lips. Fearless
and open-minded in the face of what remain the
most difficult issues of the land—the environment,
labor, the economy, politics, religion, war, justice—
Whitman found his voice in singing the voices of
the masses, and the single individual, and the road,
and the blades of grass.

Whitman is the great American poet. Yet he is a world poet too, a cosmic traveler tracing the course of stars and planets reflected in lakes, rivers, eyes and bloodstreams. To set out afoot and light-hearted with him is to venture beyond every single one of our accepted sensibilities into a sensual world in which Whitman wraps his arm around our waist like an embracing vine and leads on. He may walk beside, but he whispers a warning: "Not I, not any one else can travel that road for you, You must travel it for yourself."[2] So, be at once carefree and careful, he is not a companion for the faint of heart or weak of constitution. Whitman makes trespassers of us, beckoning us to hop the fences of political, religious and social values, crossing fields into more organic beds.

For him, Nature, including human nature, was alive and sexual. He impregnates; She gives birth; together they nurture us to our full stature. The wild Whitman and his lover Earth open our eyes to the fecundity and joy of wild intercourse; androgynous Nature teaches and guides; S/He is present at death and welcomes each of her children back into sacred soil. For Whitman, the ground below us is our fertile grounding–in exploring it with all our senses we discover our rooted being and our call to wild adventure beyond all boundaries.

Leaves of Grass, Whitman's great planting of poems, scattered fertile seeds across the continent 100 years before I was born. The year was 1855 and Walt was just thirty-six. Emerson, Thoreau, Fuller and their tribe were fertilizing the intellect of New and Old England, drawing the unsettled minds of a still-settling country beyond ancient walls of belief with their transcendental ideas. In July of 1855, Emerson received his copy of Leaves of Grass. Waldo found it "American to the bone," and quickly wrote

Whitman with high praise: "I find it the most extraordinary piece of wit and wisdom that America has yet contributed."[3] When the book was published, John Muir, Scotland's native naturalist, was digging wells, gathering crops and crafting wooden inventions on his Wisconsin farm, about to set out for the "university of the wilderness." As tribal people had always lived and honored the land, the new crop of Americans were kneeling and kneading the rich soil of a land they would all need to share, discovering new contours along unfenced lines in the emerging virgin matrix of a young and free America. Whitman's *grasses* undulated across the land greening with pioneers and poets—watered by inner rivers that still lap in coolness at our contemporary 21st-century feet.

"Look for me under your bootsoles" scribbled Walt in the last section of "Song of Myself."[4] One with the earth, the mud, with grass caked up into all creases and crevasses, staining his (and our) hands, pants, inner being. That's Walt. He's close. He wants to be. He lusts for life in the here and now. You can smell him. You have to. You have no choice. He's here, permeating the air with the scent of lilacs mingled with that of compost and blood. "We are what the atmosphere is, transparent, receptive, pervious, impervious..."[5] Take a deep draught of breath, suck in Walt along with Life, God, Nature —all that you are and are to be. Check your boots.

The Poet Universal trekked his open road singing his "songs," edited over a lifetime spanning nearly the entire 19th century. The composer of songs sprinkled the notes of the score over the pages of the land like dandelion seeds marked with gossamer threads. From the young New Yorker we hear melodies and almost operatic compositions that present a very real human being. In high moments

of ecstatic outburst he sings with an exuberant "war-ble" and "yawp," and in other, moodier moments, he sings the chants and dirges that balance the emotional state. At times he sings solitary as a soloist with a healthy blend of loneliness *and* complete fulfillment. At other times he sings with the mighty chorus of all laborers, or all suffering slaves, or all armies, or all "children of adam [and eve]"—swelling his lungs with all creation.

One beauty of Whitman is precisely this balancing that centers on singing out the truth, though a hard truth it may be. And he is unflinching in the admission of his own frailty and limitation. "With peals of distant ironical laughter at every word I have written, Pointing in silence to these songs, and then to the sand beneath. I perceive I have not really understood any thing..."[6] This is his great strength, to sing honestly and to admit his weakness, to be an intimately humble human made of the humus. Ah, but Walt never stops there! He is equally an arrogant, self-celebrating soul. After all, he is a god and a mouse, for a god can wander the streets and a mouse can "stagger sex-tillion infidels."[7]

Whitman is a true and faithful companion, a friend, a heretic who wasn't afraid to love and celebrate his body, the earthiness of it all, the land, the commonest of people, the plants and leaves, the cosmos. Earth Chaplain, Nature Saint, lightly slipping over the tangling obstacles of immovable, barbed-wired religion—sacred saunterer with sacrilege seeping in and through. Walt Whitman—I always want him on my trails. I think you will too, because you and I actually meant something to that long-ago poet-pilgrim. "And you that shall cross from shore to shore years hence, are more to me, and more in my meditations, than you might suppose..."[8] He felt no separation from the ground or

from us. We are of the same earth, the same spirit, on this common island of wonder.

As I write this, I am sitting in an early evening field of grass and stones (on a shorter isle, opposite coast from the Long Island of WW's birth), surrounded by alders and firs, croaking tree frogs and scolding squirrels. The sun is no longer warming me through the rain-blessed autumn leaves. A chill is descending. A dram warms, but not quite enough. Soon I'll carry Walt into my tiny rustic cabin in the woods and light the lamp and a candle. I am carried by Walt as well. He'd love it here. Whether planted on this weather-etched island or in a tree, climbing a forested trail to the clouds, flying the planet or lying with a lover—I need Walt Whitman, as I have needed him for nearly thirty years.

I invite you, urge you, to read his complete poems, which harbor the selections here. Let the collected rivulets lead you to the full and dancing river flowing from WW's spirit. For the most part, the readings in this book are arranged so the reader can easily find the selection sequentially within the context of *Leaves of Grass*.

Within the leaves of this book, these sheets of natural matter sprinkled with ink, I'm lifting my shoe sole and my natural soul with the poet, with you. The planet reflects his image, the earth, his "likeness," and it is a mirror of you and me. In your personal meditations, you may feel a likeness as well. We may feel the enchanted childlikeness described by Whitman when he wrote of the young one who "went forth every day, And the first object he look'd upon, that object he became," who "now goes, and will always go forth every day."[9] In this nascent spirit we are invited to be carried in the current of this lively living world, a flowing that joins

xxix

with the rich brown streams that silt and settle into the road, the trail, the open and present path with Walt.

~ Chris Highland
Whidbey Island, Washington
Winter 2004

1. "Song of the Open Road." Stanza 1.
2. "Song of Myself." Stanza 46.
3. Robert D. Richardson, Jr. *Emerson: The Mind On Fire.* University of California Press, 1995, p. 527.
4. "Song of Myself." Stanza 52.
5. "We Two, How Long We Were Fool'd". (Children of Adam). Selection 4.
6. "As I Ebb'd With the Ocean of Life." Stanza 2.
7. "Song of Myself." Stanza 31. Selection 10.
8. "Crossing Brooklyn Ferry." Stanza 1. Selection 15.
9. "There Was A Child Went Forth." (Autumn Rivulets).

A Note on Poetic Selection

As in my first three collections of John Muir, Henry David Thoreau and Ralph Waldo Emerson, it is first and foremost my intent to select historical writings, particularly literature, that celebrates Nature, and place on the page something to meditate upon (always hoping that each reader will seek out the complete works of these inspired teachers). I am well aware of the pitfalls, even offense, of excerpting selections from longer poems. My own poetry holds a certain cohesion in each piece that would lose something by excising portions for another purpose. So I proceed with great reticence, understanding that fellow poets might be uncomfortable with what I have done with Whitman's poems here. Against the purists I have perhaps sinned. But, I would suggest, not against Walt himself.

This is a spiritual exercise for me: drawing out a tidbit from the heart of a passage, wading in the river of words and stooping to enclose my hand around a stone near to the soul of the author's meaning. Meanings are often subjective, of course. Yet it appears that many who have read my other collections discover similar meanings in their own streams as they reflect upon the grander scribblings of the famous.

For the last twenty-five-odd years, as I have carried my tattered and worn copy of *Leaves of Grass* in my pack and pocket, I have often reached into those pages, nabbed a line or two, and felt the presence of a fellow "Earth Chaplain." Whitman was not ashamed

of his radical, rooted and ragged faith. Whitman's philosophy of life, which practiced an osmosis of body and soul, material and spiritual, was a *faith in the essential earthy goodness of human nature*. He saw life and lived it in an unedited and surely an uncensored manner. That is, he kept all his senses open to the breadth and depth of life without feeling he needed to edit anything out. However, he constantly sifted through what he saw and read to glean the stalks of grass that spoke to him. It is the best a poet can do and essential to the best poetry.

To one collector of his "leaves" late in life, Whitman said, "In the long run the world will do as it pleases with the book. I am determined to have the world know what I was pleased to do." He once wrote, "My poems when complete should be a *unity*, in the same sense that the earth is, or that the human body...or that a perfect musical composition is." (quotes from the Introduction, in *Complete Poetry and Selected Prose* by Walt Whitman, Houghton Mifflin, edited by James E. Miller, Jr., 1959). In that good spirit I hope the reader will pick up the tune of Whitman's work in each of these short selections.

1

Traveling Souls

Allons!* whoever you are come travel with me!
Traveling with me you find what never tires.

The earth never tires,
The earth rude, silent, incomprehensible at first,
Nature is rude and incomprehensible at first,
Be not discouraged, keep on, there are divine things
   well envelop'd,
I swear to you there are divine things more beautiful
   than words can tell.

Allons! we must not stop here,
However sweet these laid-up stores, however
   convenient this dwelling we cannot remain here,
However shelter'd this port and however calm these
   waters we must not anchor here,
However welcome the hospitality that surrounds us we
   are permitted to receive it but a little while.

*Let's go! (French)

"[We are on the river] to clear the road, remove every obstruction, and make it a road of peace."

~ Meriwether Lewis
Lewis and Clark Among the Indians, James Ronda

2

Earth, My Likeness

Earth, my likeness,
Though you look so impassive, ample and spheric there,
I now suspect that is not all;
I now suspect there is something fierce in you eligible to burst forth, for an athlete is enamor'd of me, and I of him,
But toward him there is something fierce and terrible in me eligible to burst forth,
I dare not tell it in words, not even in these songs.

"For those who find their pleasure out-of-doors ...
all the years of existence represent a long love affair with the earth,
this earth, the only earth we know."

~ Edwin Way Teale
A Naturalist Buys an Old Farm

3

World Garden

To the garden the world anew ascending,
Potent mates, daughters, sons, preluding,
The love, the life of their bodies, meaning and being,
Curious here behold my resurrection after slumber,
The revolving cycles in their wide sweep having
    brought me again,
Amorous, mature, all beautiful to me, all wondrous,
My limbs and the quivering fire that ever plays through
    them, for reasons, most wondrous,
Existing I peer and penetrate still,
Content with the present, content with the past,
By my side or back of me Eve following,
Or in front, and I following her just the same.

"God was as real to me then as the wind that rustled through the trees in our garden. God somehow cared for a magical world, full of fascinating animals and people.... It was an enchanted world for me, full of joy and wonder, and I felt very much a part of it."

~ Jane Goodall
Reason for Hope

4

Fools

We two, how long we were fool'd,
Now transmuted, we swiftly escape as Nature escapes,
We are Nature, long have we been absent, but now we
    return,
We become plants, trunks, foliage, roots, bark,
We are bedded in the ground, we are rocks,
We are oaks, we grow in the openings side by side,
We browse, we are two among the wild herds
    spontaneous as any...
. . . .
We are seas mingling, we are two of those cheerful
    waves rolling over each other and interwetting each
    other,
We are what the atmosphere is, transparent, receptive,
    pervious, impervious,
We are snow, rain, cold, darkness, we are each product
    and influence of the globe,
We have circled and circled till we have arrived home
    again, we too,
We have voided all but freedom and all but our own
    joy.

*"So may this seed germinate in your heart,
God's secret hiding place,
and through God's mysterious virtue
throw out branches, leaves, flowers and fruit."*

~ Jean-Pierre de Caussade
Sacrament of the Present Moment

5

Roots & Leaves

Roots and leaves themselves alone are these,
Scents brought to men and women from the wild
    woods and pond-side,
Breast-sorrel and pinks of love, fingers that wind
    around tighter than vines,
Gushes from the throats of birds hid in the foliage of
    trees as the sun is risen,
Breezes of land and love sent from living shores to you
    on the living sea, to you O sailors!
Frost-mellow'd berries and Third-month twigs offer'd
    fresh to young persons wandering out in the fields
    when the winter breaks up,
Love-buds put before you and within you whoever
    you are,
Buds to be unfolded on the old terms,
If you bring the warmth of the sun to them they will
    open and bring form, color, perfume, to you,
If you become the aliment and the wet they will
    become flowers, fruits, tall branches and trees.

*"You will be like the tree of life.
Your leaves, trunk, branches,
and the blossoms of your soul
will be fresh and beautiful,
once you enter the practice of
Earth Touching."*

~ Thich Nhat Hanh
The Long Road Turns to Joy

6

Formed From This Soil

I celebrate myself, and sing myself,
And what I assume you shall assume,
For every atom belonging to me as good belongs to
   you.

I loafe and invite my soul,
I lean and loafe at my ease observing a spear of summer
   grass.

My tongue, every atom of my blood, form'd from this
   soil, this air,
Born here of parents born here from parents the same,
   and their parents the same,
I, now thirty-seven years old in perfect health begin,
Hoping to cease not till death.

Creeds and schools in abeyance,
Retiring back a while sufficed at what they are, but
   never forgotten,
I harbor for good or bad, I permit to speak at every
   hazard,
Nature without check with original energy.

"I feel very humble just now … And I see no divine person.
I myself am more divine than any I see."

~ Margaret Fuller
Letter to Ralph Waldo Emerson, March 1, 1838

7

What Is The Grass?

A child said *What is the grass?* fetching it to me with full
   hands,
How could I answer the child? I do not know what it is
   any more than he.

I guess it must be the flag of my disposition, out of
   hopeful green stuff woven.

Or I guess it is the handkerchief of the Lord,
A scented gift and remembrancer designedly dropt,
Bearing the owner's name someway in the corners, that
   we may see and remark, and say *Whose?*

Or I guess the grass is itself a child, the produced babe
   of the vegetation.
. . . .

And now it seems to me the beautiful uncut hair of
   graves.
. . . .

What do you think has become of the young and old
   men?
And what do you think has become of the women and
   children?

They are alive and well somewhere,
The smallest sprout shows there is really no death, and
    if ever there was it led forward life, and does not wait
    at the end to arrest it,
And ceas'd the moment life appear'd.

All goes onward and outward, nothing collapses,
And to die is different from what any one supposed,
    and luckier.

"We measure grasses by our own stature
and the height and bulkiness of trees.
But what is the size of the greatest person,
or the tallest tree that ever overtopped a grass!"

~ John Muir
A Thousand-Mile Walk to the Gulf

8

Caressing Life

In me the caresser of life wherever moving, backward as
    well as forward sluing,
To niches aside and junior bending, not a person or
    object missing,
Absorbing all to myself and for this song.

Oxen that rattle the yoke and chain or halt in the leafy
    shade, what is that you express in your eyes?
It seems to me more than all the print I have read in
    my life.

My tread scares the wood-drake and wood-duck on my
    distant and day-long ramble,
They rise together, they slowly circle around.

I believe in those wing'd purposes,
And acknowledge red, yellow, white, playing within
    me,
And consider green and violet and the tufted crown
    intentional,
And do not call the tortoise unworthy because she is
    not something else,
And the jay in the woods never studied the gamut, yet
    trills pretty well to me,
And the look of the bay mare shames silliness out
    of me.

. . . .

The press of my foot to the earth springs a hundred affections,
They scorn the best I can do to relate them.

"The beauty [of the past]
is like the enchanted purity of late autumn,
when the leaves, though one breath would make them fall,
still glow against the sky in golden glory."

~ Bertrand Russell
A Free Man's Worship

9

Earth Lover

I am he that walks with the tender and growing night,
I call to the earth and sea half-held by the night.

Press close bare-bosom'd night—press close magnetic
    nourishing night!
Night of south winds—night of the large few stars!
Still nodding night—mad naked summer night.

Smile O voluptuous cool-breath'd earth!
Earth of the slumbering and liquid trees!
Earth of departed sunset—earth of the mountains
    misty-topt!
Earth of the vitreous pour of the full moon just tinged
    with blue!
Earth of shine and dark mottling the tide of the river!
Earth of the limpid gray of clouds brighter and clearer
    for my sake!
Far-swooping elbow'd earth—rich apple-blossom'd
    earth!
Smile, for your lover comes.

Prodigal, you have given me love—therefore I to you
    give love!
O unspeakable passionate love.

"*Where has nature spread so rich a mantle under the eye?*
mountains, forests, rocks, rivers ...
How sublime to look down into the workhouse of nature,
to see her clouds, hail, snow, rain, thunder,
all fabricated at our feet!"

~ Thomas Jefferson
Letter to Maria Cosway, Paris, October 12, 1786

10

Perspective

All truths wait in all things,
They neither hasten their own delivery nor resist it,
They do not need the obstetric forceps of the surgeon,
The insignificant is as big to me as any,
(What is less or more than a touch?).

Logic and sermons never convince,
The damp of the night drives deeper into my soul.

. . . .

I believe a leaf of grass is no less than the journey-work
    of the stars,
And the pismire is equally perfect, and a grain of sand,
    and the egg of the wren,
And the tree-toad is a chef-d'oeuvre for the highest,
And the running blackberry would adorn the parlors
    of heaven,
And the narrowest hinge in my hand puts to scorn all
    machinery,
And the cow crunching with depress'd head surpasses
    any statue,
And a mouse is miracle enough to stagger sextillions of
    infidels.

"Worlds can be found by a child and an adult bending down and looking together under the grass stems or at the skittering crabs in a tidal pool."

~Mary Catherine Bateson
With a Daughter's Eye

11

Anima — Animal

I think I could turn and live with animals, they're so
    placid and self-contain'd,
I stand and look at them long and long.

They do not sweat and whine about their condition,
They do not lie awake in the dark and weep for their
    sins,
They do not make me sick discussing their duty to God,
Not one is dissatisfied, not one is demented with the
    mania of owning things,
Not one kneels to another, nor to his kind that lived
    thousands of years ago,
Not one is respectable or unhappy over the whole
    earth.

So they show their relations to me and I accept them,
They bring me tokens of myself, they evince them
    plainly in their possession.

I wonder where they get those tokens,
Did I pass that way huge times ago and negligently
    drop them?

*"So the old people laugh
when they hear talk about the 'desecration' of the earth,
because humankind, they know,
is nothing in comparison to the earth."*

~ Leslie Marmon Silko
Pueblo Nation
Yellow Woman and a Beauty of the Spirit

12

What Do You See Walt Whitman?

What do you see Walt Whitman?
Who are they you salute, and that one after another
  salute you?

I see a great round wonder rolling through space,
I see diminute farms, hamlets, ruins, graveyards, jails,
  factories, palaces, hovels, huts of barbarians, tents of
  nomads upon the surface,
I see the shaded part on one side where the sleepers are
  sleeping, and the sunlit part on the other side,
I see the curious rapid change of the light and shade,
I see distant lands, as real and near to the inhabitants
  of them as my land is to me.

I see plenteous waters,
I see mountain peaks....

  .   .   .   .

My spirit has pass'd in compassion and determination
  around the whole earth,
I have look'd for equals and lovers and found them
  ready for me in all lands,
I think some divine rapport has equalized me with
  them.

You vapors, I think I have risen with you, moved away
    to distant continents, and fallen down there,
    for reasons,
I think I have blown with you you winds;
You waters I have finger'd every shore with you,
I have run through what any river or strait of the globe
has run through.
I have taken my stand on the bases of peninsulas and
    on the high embedded rocks, to cry thence:
Salut au monde!

"God puts things like that out there for all of us to look at.
It is just too bad that most people don't see what is really there,
and why."

~Terry Grosz
For Love of Wildness

13

Inhaling

From this hour I ordain myself loos'd of limits and
    imaginary lines,
Going where I list, my own master total and absolute,
Listening to others, considering well what they say,
Pausing, searching, receiving, contemplating,
Gently, but with undeniable will, divesting myself of
    the holds that would hold me.

I inhale great draughts of space,
The east and the west are mine, and the north and the
    south are mine.

I am larger, better than I thought,
I did not know I held so much goodness.

All seems beautiful to me,
I can repeat over to men and women
You have done such good to me I would do the same
    to you,
I will recruit for myself and you as I go,
I will scatter myself among men and women as I go,
I will toss a new gladness and roughness among them,
Whoever denies me it shall not trouble me,
Whoever accepts me he or she shall be blessed and shall
    bless me.

"He walked and he walked, and the earth and the holiness of the earth came up through the soles of his feet."

~ Gretel Ehrlich
Legacy of Light

14

The Float of Things

Now if a thousand perfect men were to appear it would
    not amaze me,
Now if a thousand beautiful forms of women appear'd
    it would not astonish me.

Now I see the secret of the making of the best persons,
It is to grow in the open air and to eat and sleep with
    the earth.

Here a great personal deed has room,
(Such a deed seizes upon the hearts of the whole race
    of men,
Its effusion of strength and will overwhelms law and
    mocks all authority and all argument against it.)

Here is the test of wisdom,
Wisdom is not finally tested in schools,
Wisdom cannot be pass'd from one having it to anoth-
    er not having it,
Wisdom is of the soul, is not susceptible of proof, is its
    own proof,
Applies to all stages and objects and qualities and is
    content,
Is the certainty of the reality and immortality of things,
    and the excellence of things;
Something there is in the float of the sight of things
    that provokes it out of the soul.

Now I re-examine philosophies and religions,
They may prove well in lecture-rooms, yet not prove
   at all under the spacious clouds and along the
   landscape and flowing currents.

"The Way is empty;
Yet when you use it, you never need fill it again.
Like an abyss!
It seems to be the ancestor of the ten thousand things."

~ Lao Tzu
Tao Te Ching

15

Flow On, River, Flow

Flood-tide below me! I see you face to face!
Clouds of the west—sun there half an hour high—
I see you also face to face.

Crowds of men and women attired in the usual
  costumes, how curious you are to me!
On the ferry-boats the hundreds and hundreds that
  cross, returning home, are more curious to me than
  you suppose,
And you that shall cross from shore to shore years
  hence are more to me, and more in my meditations,
  than you might suppose.

.   .   .   .

What gods can exceed these that clasp me by the hand,
  and with voices I love call me promptly and loudly
  by my nighest name as I approach?

.   .   .   .

Flow on, river! flow with the flood-tide, and ebb with
  the ebb-tide!
Frolic on, crested and scallop-edg'd waves!
Gorgeous clouds of the sunset! drench with your
  splendor me, or the men and women generations
  after me!
Cross from shore to shore, countless crowds of
  passengers!

Stand up, tall masts of Mannahatta! stand up, beautiful
   hills of Brooklyn!
Throb, baffled and curious brain! throw out questions
   and answers!
Suspend here and everywhere, eternal float of solution!
.   .   .   .

Thrive, cities—bring your freight, bring your shows,
   ample and sufficient rivers,
Expand, being than which none else is perhaps more
   spiritual.

*"Sometimes we'd have that whole river all to ourselves
for the longest time."*

~ Mark Twain
Huckleberry Finn

16

Myriads Unnoticed

Always the free range and diversity—always the
    continent of Democracy;
Always the prairies, pastures, forests, vast cities,
    travelers,
Kanada, the snows;
Always these compact lands tied at the hips with the
    belt stringing the huge oval lakes;
Always the West with strong native persons, the
    increasing density there, the habitans, friendly,
    threatening, ironical, scorning invaders;
All sights, South, North, East—all deeds promiscuously
    done at all times,
All characters, movements, growths, a few noticed,
    myriads unnoticed ...

. . . .

The hawk sailing where men have not yet sail'd, the
    farthest polar sea, ripply, crystalline, open, beyond
    the floes,
White drift spooning ahead where the ship in the
    tempest dashes,
On solid land what is done in cities as the bells strike
    midnight together,
In primitive woods the sounds there also sounding, the
    howl of the wolf, the scream of the panther, and the
    hoarse bellow of the elk ...

. . . .

Singing the song of These, my ever-united lands—
    my body no more inevitably united, part to part,
    and made out of a thousand diverse contributions
    one identity, any more than my lands are inevitably
    united and made
ONE IDENTITY.

*"Probably all the organic beings which have ever lived on this earth
have descended from some one primordial form,
into which life was first breathed."*

~Charles Darwin
The Origin of Species

17

O The Joy

O to make the most jubilant song!
Full of music—full of manhood, womanhood, infancy!
Full of common employments—full of grain and trees.

O for the voices of animals—O for the swiftness and
  balance of fishes!
O for the dropping of raindrops in a song!
O for the sunshine and motion of waves in a song!

O the joy of my spirit—it is uncaged—it darts like
  lightning!
It is not enough to have this globe or a certain time,
I will have thousands of globes and all time.

.   .   .   .

O the gleesome saunter over fields and hillsides!
The leaves and flowers of the commonest weeds, the
  moist fresh stillness of the woods,
The exquisite smell of the earth at daybreak, and all
  through the forenoon.

.   .   .   .

What beauty is this that descends upon me and rises
  out of me?

.   .   .   .

To be indeed a God!

O to sail to sea in a ship!
To leave this steady unendurable land,
To leave the tiresome sameness of the streets, the
  sidewalks and the houses,

To leave you O you solid motionless land, and entering
a ship,
To sail and sail and sail!

O to have life henceforth a poem of new joys!
To dance, clap hands, exult, shout, skip, leap, roll on,
float on!
To be a sailor of the world bound for all ports,
A ship itself, (see indeed these sails I spread to the sun
and air,)
A swift and swelling ship full of rich words, full of joys.

"The Gods of the earth and sea,
Sought thro' Nature to find this Tree;
But their search was all in vain,
There grows one in the Human Brain."

~ William Blake
Songs of Innocence and of Experience

18

Common Destiny

Long and long has the green been growing,
Long and long has the rain been falling,
Long has the globe been rolling round.

.   .   .   .

The male and female many laboring not,
Shall ever here confront the laboring many,
With precious benefits to both, glory to all,
To thee America, and thee eternal Muse.

And here shall ye inhabit powerful Matrons!
In your vast state vaster than all the old,
Echoed through long, long centuries to come,
To sound of different, prouder songs, with stronger
    themes,
Practical, peaceful life, the people's life, the People
    themselves,
Lifted, illumin'd, bathed in peace—elate, secure in
    peace.

Away with themes of war! away with war itself!

.   .   .   .

And thou America,
Thy offspring towering e'er so high, yet higher Thee
    above all towering,
With Victory on thy left, and at thy right hand Law;
Thou Union holding all, fusing, absorbing, tolerating all,
Thee, ever thee, I sing.

Thou, also thou, a World,
With all thy wide geographies, manifold, different,
   distant,
Rounded by thee in one—one common orbic language,
One common indivisible destiny for All.

"*The love of one's country is a splendid natural thing.
But why should love stop at the border...?
We are all leaves of a tree, and the tree is humanity.* "

~ Pablo Casals
Joys and Sorrows

19

Chant of The Seasons And Time

A California song,
A prophecy and indirection, a thought impalpable to
    breathe as air,
A chorus of dryads, fading, departing, or hamadryads
    departing,
A murmuring, fateful, giant voice, out of the earth and
    sky,
Voice of a mighty dying tree in the redwood forest
    dense.

Farewell my brethren,
Farewell O earth and sky, farewell ye neighboring waters,
My time has ended, my term has come.

Along the northern coast,
Just back from the rock-bound shore and the caves,
In the saline air from the sea in the Mendocino
    country,
With the surge for base and accompaniment low and
    hoarse,
With crackling blows of axes sounding musically driven
    by strong arms,
Riven deep by the sharp tongues of the axes, there in
    the redwood forest dense,
I heard the mighty tree its death-chant chanting.

The choppers heard not, the camp shanties echoed not,
The quick-ear'd teamsters and chain and jack-screw
    men heard not,
As the wood-spirits came from their haunts of a
    thousand years to join the refrain,
But in my soul I plainly heard.

Murmuring out of its myriad leaves,
Down from its lofty top rising two hundred feet high,
Out of its stalwart trunk and limbs, out of its foot-thick
    bark,
That chant of the seasons and time, chant not of the
    past only but the future.

You untold life of me,
And all you venerable and innocent joys,
Perennial hardy life of me with joys 'mid rain and many a summer
    sun,
And the white snows and night and the wild winds;
O the great patient rugged joys, my soul's strong joys unreck'd by
    man,
(For know I bear the soul befitting me, I too have
    consciousness, identity,
And all the rocks and mountains have, and all the earth,)
Joys of the life befitting me and brothers mine,
Our time, our term has come.

Nor yield we mournfully majestic brothers,
We who have grandly fill'd our time;
With Nature's calm content, with tacit huge delight,
We welcome what we wrought for through the past,
And leave the field for them.

"The very look of the land makes one long to keep it intact—
the spiritual reserve of a few bright spirits."

~ Henry Miller
Big Sur

20

Apple-Shaped Earth

There is something that comes to one now and
    perpetually,
It is not what is printed, preach'd, discussed, it eludes
    discussion and print,
It is not to be put in a book, it is not in this book,
It is for you whoever you are, it is no farther from you
    than your hearing and sight are from you,
It is hinted by nearest, commonest, readiest, it is ever
    provoked by them.

You may read in many languages, yet read nothing
    about it,
You may read the President's message and read nothing
    about it there,
Nothing in the reports from the State department or
    Treasury department, or in the daily papers or week-
    ly papers,
Or in the census of revenue returns, prices current, or
    any accounts of stock.

The sun and stars that float in the open air,
The apple-shaped earth and we upon it, surely the drift
    of them is something grand,
I do not know what it is except that it is grand, and
    that it is happiness,
And that the enclosing purport of us here is not a
    speculation or bon-mot or reconnoissance,
And it is not something which by luck may turn out
    well for us, and without luck must be a failure for us,
And not something which may yet be retracted in a
    certain contingency.

The light and shade, the curious sense of body and
    identity, the greed that with perfect complaisance
    devours all things,
The endless pride and outstretching of man,
    unspeakable joys and sorrows,
The wonder every one sees in every one else he sees,
    and the wonders that fill each minute of time
    forever,
What have you reckon'd them for, camerado?

.   .   .   .

We consider bibles and religion divine—I do not say
    they are not divine,
I say they have all grown out of you, and may grow out
    of you still,
It is not they who give the life, it is you who give the
    life,
Leaves are not more shed from the trees, or trees from
    the earth, than they are shed out of you.

"It is not easy to see how the more extreme forms of nationalism
        can long survive when men begin to see the Earth
    in its true perspective as a single small globe among the stars."

~Arthur C. Clarke
The Challenge of the Spaceship

21

Workshop Of Souls

A song of the rolling earth, and of words according,
Were you thinking that those were the words, those
    upright lines? those curves, angles, dots?
No, those are not the words, the substantial words are
    in the ground and sea,
They are in the air, they are in you.

Were you thinking that those were the words, those
    delicious sounds out of your friends' mouths?
No, the real words are more delicious than they.

Human bodies are words, myriads of words,
(In the best poems re-appears the body, man's or
    woman's, well-shaped, natural, gay,
Every part able, active, receptive, without shame or the
    need of shame.)

Air, soil, water, fire—those are words,
I myself am a word with them—my qualities
    interpenetrate with theirs—my name is nothing
    to them,
Though it were told in the three thousand languages,
    what would air, soil, water, fire, know of my name?

A healthy presence, a friendly or commanding gesture,
    are words, sayings, meanings,
The charms that go with the mere looks of some men
    and women, are sayings and meanings also.

The workmanship of souls is by those inaudible words
   of the earth,
The masters know the earth's words and use them
   more than audible words.

"Our lack of intimacy with each other is in direct proportion to our
lack of intimacy with the land. We have taken our love inside and
abandoned the wild."

~ Terry Tempest Williams
An Unspoken Hunger

22

I Swear

I swear the earth shall surely be complete to him or her
    who shall be complete,
The earth remains jagged and broken only to him or
    her who remains jagged and broken.

I swear there is no greatness or power that does not
    emulate those of the earth,
There can be no theory of any account unless it
    corroborate the theory of the earth,
No politics, song, religion, behavior, or what not, is of
    account, unless it compare with the amplitude of
    the earth,
Unless it face the exactness, vitality, impartiality,
    rectitude of the earth.

I swear I begin to see love with sweeter spasms than
    that which responds love,
It is that which contains itself, which never invites and
    never refuses.

I swear I begin to see little or nothing in audible words,
All merges toward the presentation of the unspoken
    meanings of the earth,
Toward him who sings the songs of the body and of
    the truths of the earth,
Toward him who makes the dictionaries of words that
    print cannot touch.

I swear I see what is better than to tell the best,
It is always to leave the best untold.

When I undertake to tell the best I find I cannot,
My tongue is ineffectual on its pivots,
My breath will not be obedient to its organs,
I become a dumb man.

"To the extent that a well is of use
when there is a flood of water on all sides,
to the same extent are all the [scriptures] of use
to an enlightened [one]."

~ Bhagavad Gita 2:46
Bhagavad Gita According to Gandhi

23

The Seed Is Waiting

Come said the Muse,
Sing me a song no poet yet has chanted,
Sing me the universal.

In this broad earth of ours,
Amid the measureless grossness and the slag,
Enclosed and safe within its central heart,
Nestles the seed perfection.

By every life a share or more or less,
None born but it is born, conceal'd or unconceal'd the
   seed is waiting.

.   .   .   .

All, all for immortality,
Love like the light silently wrapping all,
Nature's amelioration blessing all,
The blossoms, fruits of ages, orchards divine and certain,
Forms, objects, growths, humanities, to spiritual images
   ripening.

Give me O God to sing that thought,
Give me, give him or her I love this quenchless faith,
In Thy ensemble, whatever else withheld withhold not
   from us,
Belief in plan of Thee enclosed in Time and Space,
Health, peace, salvation universal.

Is it a dream?
Nay but the lack of it the dream,
And failing it life's lore and wealth a dream,
And all the world a dream.

"If then God so clothe the grass ...
how much more will he clothe you?"

~ Jesus of Nazareth
Luke 12:28 (The Jefferson Bible)

24

Walking The Walk Of Dreams

Whoever you are, I fear you are walking the walk of
   dreams,
I fear these supposed realities are to melt from under
   your feet and hands,
Even now your features, joys, speech, house, trade,
   manners, troubles, follies, costume, crimes, dissipate
   away from you,
Your true soul and body appear before me,
They stand forth out of affairs, out of commerce, shops,
   work, farms, clothes, the house, buying, selling,
   eating, drinking, suffering, dying.

Whoever you are, now I place my hand upon you, that
   you be my poem,
I whisper with my lips close to your ear,
I have loved many women and men, but I love none
   better than you.

O I have been dilatory and dumb,
I should have made my way straight to you long ago,
I should have blabb'd nothing but you, I should have
   chanted nothing but you.

I will leave all and come and make the hymns of you,
None has understood you, but I understand you,
None has done justice to you, you have not done
    justice to yourself,
None but has found you imperfect, I only find no
    imperfection in you,
None but would subordinate you, I only am he who
    will never consent to subordinate you,
I only am he who places over you no master, owner,
    better, God, beyond what waits intrinsically in
    yourself.

"As I walked through the wilderness of this world,
I lighted on a certain place where was a den,
and I laid me down in that place to sleep:
and as I slept, I dreamed a dream."

~ John Bunyan
The Pilgrim's Progess

25

Island Shore

As I ebb'd with the ocean of life,
As I wended the shores I know,
As I walk'd where the ripples continually wash you
    Paumanok,
Where they rustle up hoarse and sibilant,
Where the fierce old mother endlessly cries for her
    castaways,
I musing late in the autumn day, gazing off southward,
Held by this electric self out of the pride of which I
    utter poems,
Was seiz'd by the spirit that trails in the lines
    underfoot,
The rim, the sediment that stands for all the water and
    all the land of the globe.

Fascinated, my eyes reverting from the south, dropt, to
    follow those slender windrows,
Chaff, straw, splinters of wood, weeds, and the
    sea-gluten,
Scum, scales from shining rocks, leaves of salt-lettuce,
    left by the tide,
Miles walking, the sound of breaking waves the other
    side of me,
Paumanok there and then as I thought the old thought
    of likenesses,
These you presented to me you fish-shaped island,
As I wended the shores I know,
As I walk'd with that electric self seeking types.

As I wend to the shores I know not,
As I list to the dirge, the voices of men and women
    wreck'd,
As I inhale the impalpable breezes that set in upon me,
As the ocean so mysterious rolls toward me closer and
    closer,
I too but signify at the utmost a little wash'd-up drift,
A few sands and dead leaves to gather,
Gather, and merge myself as part of the sands and drift.

*"Thou ocean branch that flowest to the sun
Incense of earth, perfumed with flowers —
Spirit of lakes and rivers, seas and rills
Come to revisit now thy native scenes."*

~ Henry David Thoreau
"Fog" (Poems)

26

Trans-Parent

On the beach at night,
Stands a child with her father,
Watching the east, the autumn sky.

Up through the darkness,
While ravening clouds, the burial clouds, in black
    masses spreading,
Lower sullen and fast athwart and down the sky,
Amid a transparent clear belt of ether yet left in the
    east,
Ascends large and calm the lord-star Jupiter,
And nigh at hand, only a very little above,
Swim the delicate sisters the Pleiades.

From the beach the child holding the hand of her
    father,
Those buried clouds that lower victorious soon to
    devour all,
Watching, silently weeps.

Weep not, child,
Weep not, my darling,
With these kisses let me remove your tears,
The ravening clouds shall not long be victorious,
They shall not long possess the sky, they devour the
    stars only in apparition,
Jupiter shall emerge, be patient, watch again another
    night, the Pleiades shall emerge,
They are immortal, all those stars both silvery and
    golden shall shine out again,
The great stars and the little ones shall shine out again,
    they endure,

The vast immortal suns and the long-enduring pensive
   moons shall again shine.
.   .   .   .

On the beach at night alone,
As the old mother sways her to and fro singing her
   husky song,
As I watch the bright stars shining, I think a thought of
   the clef of the universes and of the future.
.   .   .   .

All lives and deaths, all of the past, present, future,
This vast similitude spans them, and always has
   spann'd,
And shall forever span them and compactly hold and
   enclose them.

*"The world itself is the child's cathedral, and so it may be for us
adults, if we can relearn our childlike openness to it."*

~ Philip Simmons
Learning to Fall

27

Be Thou My God

Lover divine and perfect Comrade,
Waiting content, invisible yet, but certain,
Be thou my God.

Thou, thou, the Ideal Man,
Fair, able, beautiful, content, and loving,
Complete in body and dilate in spirit,
Be thou my God.

O Death, (for Life has served its turn,)
Opener and usher to the heavenly mansion,
Be thou my God.

Aught, aught of mightiest, best I see, conceive, or know,
(To break the stagnant tie—thee, thee to free, O soul,)
Be thou my God.

All great ideas, the races' aspirations,
All heroisms, deeds of rapt enthusiasts,
Be ye my Gods.

Or Time and Space,
Or shape of Earth divine and wondrous,
Or some fair shape I viewing, worship,
Or lustrous orb of sun or star by night,
Be ye my Gods.

"For whatever of happiness is still on its way between heaven and earth now seeks a shelter in a bright soul."

~ Friedrich Nietzsche
Thus Spoke Zarathustra

28

Eagles

Skirting the river road, (my forenoon walk, my rest,)
Skyward in air a sudden muffled sound, the dalliance
   of the eagles,
The rushing amorous contact high in space together,
The clinching interlocking claws, a living, fierce,
   gyrating wheel,
Four beating wings, two beaks, a swirling mass tight
   grappling,
In tumbling turning clustering loops, straight
   downward falling,
Till o'er the river pois'd, the twain yet one, a moment's
   lull,
A motionless still balance in the air, then parting,
   talons loosing,
Upward again on slow-firm pinions slanting, their
   separate diverse flight,
She hers, he his, pursuing.

"This must be the secret of the fascination which birds hold for human beings, I told myself. To know them, but never completely to understand."

~ Florence Page Jaques
Birds Across the Sky

29

Hungering Gymnastic

Rise O days from your fathomless deeps, till you loftier, fiercer sweep,
Long for my soul hungering gymnastic I devour'd what the earth gave me,
Long I roam'd the woods of the north, long I watch'd Niagara pouring,
I travel'd the prairies over and slept on their breast, I cross'd the Nevadas,
I cross'd the plateaus,
I ascended the towering rocks along the Pacific, I sail'd out to sea,
I sail'd through the storm, I was refresh'd by the storm,
I watch'd with joy the threatening maws of the waves,
I mark'd the white combs where they career'd so high, curling over,
I heard the wind piping, I saw the black clouds,
Saw from below what arose and mounted, (O superb! O wild as my heart, and powerful!)
Heard the continuous thunder as it bellow'd after the lightning,
Noted the slender and jagged threads of lightning as sudden and fast amid the din they chased each other across the sky;
These, and such as these, I, elate saw—saw with wonder, yet pensive and masterful,
All the menacing might of the globe uprisen around me,
Yet there with my soul I fed, I fed content, supercilious.

. . . .

Hungering, hungering, hungering, for primal energies
and Nature's dauntlessness,
I refresh'd myself with it only, I could relish it only,
I waited the bursting forth of the pent, fire—on the
water and air
I waited long;
But now I no longer wait, I am fully satisfied, I am
glutted,
I have witness'd the true lightning, I have witness'd my
cities electric,
I have lived to behold man burst forth and warlike
America rise,
Hence I will seek no more the food of the northern
solitary wilds,
No more the mountains roam or sail the stormy sea.

"This is the world of the primitive, where even inanimate objects
are endowed with a living, healing, magic power,
through which they participate in us and we in them."

~ Carl Jung
Eastern and Western Thinking

30

Star Camp

I see before me now a traveling army halting,
Below a fertile valley spread, with barns and the
    orchards of summer,
Behind, the terraced sides of a mountain, abrupt, in
    places rising high,
Broken, with rocks, with clinging cedars, with tall
    shapes dingily seen,
The numerous camp-fires scatter'd near and far, some
    away up on the mountain,
The shadowy forms of men and horses, looming, large-
    sized, flickering,
And over all the sky—the sky! far, far out of reach,
    studded, breaking out, the eternal stars.

*"If you study what the Creator has put here on earth,
you will learn many things. The earth has much to teach us."*

~ Vi Hilbert
Upper Skagit Tribe
Messengers of the Wind

31

At The Foot Of A Tree

As toilsome I wander'd Virginia's woods,
To the music of rustling leaves kick'd by my feet,
    (for 'twas autumn,)
I mark'd at the foot of a tree the grave of a soldier;
Mortally wounded he and buried on the retreat, (easily
    all could I understand,)
The halt of a mid-day hour, when up! no time to lose
    —yet this sign left,
On a tablet scrawl'd and nail'd on the tree by the grave,
Bold, cautious, true, and my loving comrade.

Long, long I muse, then on my way go wandering,
Many a changeful season to follow, and many a scene
    of life,
Yet at times through changeful season and scene,
    abrupt, alone, or in the crowded street,
Comes before me the unknown soldier's grave, comes
    the inscription rude in Virginia's woods,
Bold, cautious, true, and my loving comrade.

"The old tree is very wise, it sees that much of the world's business is great foolishness ... I always find a more cheerful atmosphere, and a more sensible aspect to my folly, under the shadow of this friend of mine."

~ Sarah Orne Jewett
"A Winter Drive" (Country By-Ways)

32

Primal Sanity

Give me the splendid silent sun with all his beams
full-dazzling,
Give me juicy autumnal fruit ripe and red from the
orchard,
Give me a field where the unmow'd grass grows,
Give me an arbor, give me the trellis'd grape,
Give me fresh corn and wheat, give me serene-moving
animals teaching content,
Give me nights perfectly quiet as on high plateaus west
of the Mississippi, and I looking up at the stars,
Give me odorous at sunrise a garden of beautiful
flowers where I can walk undisturb'd,
Give me for marriage a sweet-breath'd woman of whom
I should never tire,
Give me a perfect child, give me away aside from the
noise of the world a rural domestic life,
Give me to warble spontaneous songs, recluse by
myself, for my own ears only,
Give me solitude, give me Nature, give me again
O Nature your primal sanities!

"When I creep out into the Night or the Morning and see what majestic and what tender beauties daily wrap me in their bosom, how near to me is every transcendent secret of Nature's love and religion, I see how indifferent it is where I eat and sleep."

~ Ralph Waldo Emerson
Journals, June 6, 1841

33

Every Leaf A Miracle

When lilacs last in the dooryard bloom'd,
And the great star early droop'd in the western sky in
the night,
I mourn'd, and yet shall mourn with ever-returning
spring.

Ever-returning spring, trinity sure to me you bring,
Lilac blooming perennial and drooping star in the west,
And thought of him I love.

O powerful western fallen star!
O shades of night—O moody, tearful night!
O great star disappear'd—O the black murk that hides
the star!
O cruel hands that hold me powerless—O helpless soul
of me!
O harsh surrounding cloud that will not free my soul.

In the dooryard fronting an old farm-house near the
white-wash'd palings,
Stands the lilac-bush tall-growing with heart-shaped
leaves of rich green,
With many a pointed blossom rising delicate, with the
perfume strong I love,
With every leaf a miracle—and from this bush in the
dooryard,

With delicate-color'd blossoms and heart-shaped leaves
    of rich green,
A sprig with its flower I break.

"Let us hope, that by the best cultivation of the physical world,
beneath and around us; and the intellectual and moral world
within us, we shall secure an individual, social, and political
prosperity and happiness... which, while the earth endures,
shall not pass away."

~ Abraham Lincoln
Address to the Wisconsin State Agricultural Society, September 30, 1859

34

O Wondrous Singer!

Sing on, sing on you gray-brown bird,
Sing from the swamps, the recesses, pour your chant
    from the bushes,
Limitless out of the dusk, out of the cedars and pines.

Sing on dearest brother, warble your reedy song,
Loud human song, with voice of uttermost woe.

O liquid and free and tender!
O wild and loose to my soul—O wondrous singer!
You only I hear—yet the star holds me, (but will soon
    depart,)
Yet the lilac with mastering odor holds me.

Now while I sat in the day and look'd forth,
In the close of the day with its light and the fields of
    spring, and the farmers preparing their crops,
In the large unconscious scenery of my land with its
    lakes and forests,
In the heavenly aerial beauty, (after the perturb'd winds
    and the storms,)
Under the arching heavens of the afternoon swift
    passing, and the voices of children and women,
The many-moving sea-tides, and I saw the ships how
    they sail'd,
And the summer approaching with richness, and the
    fields all busy with labor,
And the infinite separate houses, how they all went on,
    each with its meals and minutia of daily usages,
And the streets how their throbbings throbb'd, and the
    cities pent—lo, then and there,

Falling upon them all and among them all, enveloping
    me with the rest,
Appear'd the cloud, appear'd the long black trail,
And I knew death, its thought, and the sacred
    knowledge of death.

Then with the knowledge of death as walking one side
    of me,
And the thought of death close-walking the other side
    of me,
And I in the middle as with companions, and as
    holding the hands of companions,
I fled forth to the hiding receiving night that talks not,
Down to the shores of the water, the path by the
    swamp in the dimness,
To the solemn shadowy cedars and ghostly pines so
    still.

And the singer so shy to the rest receiv'd me,
The gray-brown bird I know receiv'd us comrades three,
And he sang the carol of death, and a verse for him
    I love.

From deep secluded recesses,
From the fragrant cedars and the ghostly pines so still,
Came the carol of the bird.

And the charm of the carol rapt me,
As I held as if by their hands my comrades in the night,
And the voice of my spirit tallied the song of the bird.

"I like to lie against the earth and whisper to it my sorrows,
my prayers."

~ Marc Chagall
My Life

35

Mystic Ocean Currents

As consequent from store of summer rains,
Or wayward rivulets in autumn flowing,
Or many a herb-lined brook's reticulations,
Or subterranean sea-rills making for the sea,
Songs of continued years I sing.

Life's ever-modern rapids first, (soon, soon to blend,
With the old streams of death.)

Some threading Ohio's farm-fields or the woods,
Some down Colorado's canons from sources of
    perpetual snow,
Some half-hid in Oregon, or away southward in Texas,
Some in the north finding their way to Erie, Niagara,
    Ottawa,
Some to Atlantica's bays, and so to the great salt brine.

In you whoe'er you are my book perusing,
In I myself, in all the world, these currents flowing,
All, all toward the mystic ocean tending.

Currents for starting a continent new,
Overtures sent to the solid out of the liquid,
Fusion of ocean and land, tender and pensive waves ...

. . . .

Will you not little shells to the tympans of temples
   held,
Murmurs and echoes still call up, eternity's music faint
   and far ...?

"There is a pleasure in the pathless woods,
There is a rapture on the lonely shore,
There is society, where none intrudes,
By the deep Sea, and music in its roar."

~ Lord Byron
Childe Harold's Pilgrimage

36

Calm Annual Drama

For the lands and for these passionate days and for
    myself,
Now I awhile retire to thee O soil of autumn fields,
Reclining on thy breast, giving myself to thee,
Answering the pulses of thy sane and equable heart,
Tuning a verse for thee.

O earth that hast no voice, confide to me a voice,
O harvest of my lands—O boundless summer growths,
O lavish brown parturient earth—O infinite teeming
    womb,
A song to narrate thee.

Ever upon this stage,
Is acted God's calm annual drama,
Gorgeous processions, songs of birds,
Sunrise that fullest feeds and freshens most the soul,
The heaving sea, the waves upon the shore,
    the musical, strong waves,
The woods, the stalwart trees, the slender, tapering
    trees,
The liliput countless armies of the grass,
The heat, the showers, the measureless pasturages,
The scenery of the snows, the winds' free orchestra,
The stretching light-hung roof of clouds, the clear
    cerulean and the silvery fringes,
The high dilating stars, the placid beckoning stars,
The moving flocks and herds, the plains and emerald
    meadows,
The shows of all the varied lands and all the growths
    and products.

But on these days of brightness,
On the far-stretching beauteous landscape, the roads
and lanes, the high-piled farm-wagons, and the
fruits and barns,
Should the dead intrude?

Ah the dead to me mar not, they fit well in Nature,
They fit very well in the landscape, under the trees
and grass,
And along the edge of the sky in the horizon's far
margin.

"Human subtlety … will never devise an invention more beautiful,
more simple or more direct than does Nature, because in her
inventions, nothing is lacking and nothing is superfluous."

~ Leonardo da Vinci
Notebooks

37

Mother Of All

Loud O my throat, and clear O soul!
The season of thanks and the voice of full-yielding,
The chant of joy and power for boundless fertility.

All till'd and untill'd fields expand before me,
I see the true arenas of my race, or first or last,
Man's innocent and strong arenas.

I see the heroes at other toils,
I see well-wielded in their hands the better weapons.

I see where the Mother of All,
With full-spanning eye gazes forth, dwells long,
And counts the varied gathering of the products.

Busy the far, the sunlit panorama,
Prairie, orchard, and yellow grain of the North,
Cotton and rice of the South and Louisianian cane,
Open unseeded fallows, rich fields of clover and
    timothy,
Kine and horses feeding, and droves of sheep and
    swine,
And many a stately river flowing and many a jocund
    brook,
And healthy uplands with herby-perfumed breezes,
And the good green grass, that delicate miracle the
    ever-recurring grass.

Toil on heroes! harvest the products!
Not alone on those warlike fields the Mother of All,
With dilated form and lambent eyes watch'd you.

Toil on heroes! toil well! handle the weapons well!
The Mother of All, yet here as ever she watches you.

"Silently I mouth my prayer to the river:
'Mother, be gentle with me'."

~ Denise Chavez
Writing Down the River: Into the Heart of the Grand Canyon

38

What Chemistry!

Behold this compost! behold it well!
Perhaps every mite has once form'd part of a sick
    person—yet behold!
The grass of spring covers the prairies,
The bean bursts noiselessly through the mould in the
    garden,
The delicate spear of the onion pierces upward,
The apple-buds cluster together on the apple-branches,
The resurrection of the wheat appears with pale visage
    out of its graves,
The tinge awakes over the willow-tree and the
    mulberry-tree,
The he-birds carol mornings and evenings while the
    she-birds sit on their nests,
The young of poultry break through the hatch'd eggs,
The new-born of animals appear, the calf is dropp'd
    from the cow, the colt from the mare,
Out of its little hill faithfully rise the potato's dark
    green leaves,
Out of its hill rises the yellow maize-stalk, the lilacs
    bloom in the dooryards,
The summer growth is innocent and disdainful above
    all those strata of sour dead.
What chemistry!
That the winds are really not infectious,
That this is no cheat, this transparent green-wash of
    the sea which is so amorous after me,
That it is safe to allow it to lick my naked body all over
    with its tongues,
That it will not endanger me with the fevers that have
    deposited themselves in it,

That all is clean forever and ever,
That the cool drink from the well tastes so good,
That blackberries are so flavorous and juicy,
That the fruits of the apple-orchard and the orange-
    orchard, that melons, grapes, peaches, plums, will
    none of them poison me,
That when I recline on the grass I do not catch any
    disease,
Though probably every spear of grass rises out of what
    was once a catching disease.
Now I am terrified at the Earth, it is that calm and
    patient,
It grows such sweet things out of such corruptions,
It turns harmless and stainless on its axis, with such
    endless successions of diseas'd corpses,
It distills such exquisite winds out of such infused
    fetor,
It renews with such unwitting looks its prodigal,
    annual, sumptuous crops,
It gives such divine materials to men, and accepts such
    leavings from them at last.

"In all things of Nature there is something of the marvelous."

~ Aristotle
Historia Animalium

39

Thou Soul Unloosen'd

Warble me now for joy of lilac-time (returning in
    reminiscence,)
Sort me O tongue and lips for Nature's sake, souvenirs
    of earliest summer,
Gather the welcome signs, (as children with pebbles or
    stringing shells,)
Put in April and May, the hylas croaking in the ponds,
    the elastic air,
Bees, butterflies, the sparrow with its simple notes,
Blue-bird and darting swallow, nor forget the high-hole
    flashing his golden wings,
The tranquil sunny haze, the clinging smoke, the vapor,
Shimmer of water with fish in them, the cerulean
    above,
All that is jocund and sparkling, the brooks running,
The maple woods, the crisp February days and the
    sugar-making,
The robin where he hops, bright-eyed, brown-breasted,
With musical clear call at sunrise, and again at sunset,
Or flitting among the trees of the apple-orchard,
    building the nest of his mate,
The melted snow of March, the willow sending forth its
    yellow-green sprouts,
For spring-time is here! the summer is here! and what
    is this in it and from it?
Thou, soul, unloosen'd—the restlessness after I know
    not what;
Come, let us lag here no longer, let us be up and away!
O if one could but fly like a bird!

O to escape, to sail forth as in a ship!
To glide with thee O soul, o'er all, in all, as a ship o'er
    the waters;
Gathering these hints, the preludes, the blue sky, the
    grass, the morning drops of dew,
The lilac-scent, the bushes with dark green heart-
    shaped leaves,
Wood-violets, the little delicate pale blossoms called
    innocence,
Samples and sorts not for themselves alone, but for
    their atmosphere,
To grace the bush I love—to sing with the birds,
A warble for joy of lilac-time, returning in reminiscence.

*"The true poet knows more about Nature than the naturalists
because he carries her open secrets in his heart."*

~ John Burroughs
Birds and Poets

40

Thy Name An Earth

What may we chant, O thou within this tomb?
What tablets, outlines, hang for thee, O millionaire?
The life thou lived'st we know not,
But that thou walk'dst thy years in barter, 'mid the
    haunts of brokers,
Nor heroism thine, nor war, nor glory.

Silent, my soul,
With drooping lids, as waiting, ponder'd,
Turning from all the samples, monuments of heroes.

All, all the shows of laboring life,
City and country, women's, men's and children's,
Their wants provided for, hued in the sun and tinged
    for once with joy ...
The student, boy or girl, led forward to be taught,
The sick cared for, the shoeless shod, the orphan
    father'd and mother'd,
The hungry fed, the houseless housed;
(The intentions perfect and divine,
The workings, details, haply human.)

O thou within this tomb,
From thee such scenes, thou stintless, lavish giver,
Tallying the gifts of earth, large as the earth,
Thy name an earth, with mountains, fields, and tides.

"What is life? It is the flash of a firefly in the night.
It is the breath of a buffalo in the wintertime.
It is the little shadow which runs across the grass
and loses itself in the sunset."

~ Crowfoot
Blackfeet Nation
"Last Words"

41

Wonderfulness

Why, who makes much of a miracle?
As to me I know of nothing else but miracles,
Whether I walk the streets of Manhattan,
Or dart my sight over the roofs of houses toward the
    sky,
Or wade with naked feet along the beach just in the
    edge of the water,
Or stand under trees in the woods,
Or talk by day with any one I love, or sleep in the bed
    at night with any one I love,
Or sit at table at dinner with the rest,
Or look at strangers opposite me riding in the car,
Or watch honey-bees busy around the hive of a
    summer forenoon,
Or animals feeding in the fields,
Or birds, or the wonderfulness of insects in the air,
Or the wonderfulness of the sundown, or of stars
    shining so quiet and bright,
Or the exquisite delicate thin curve of the new moon in
    spring;
These with the rest, one and all, are to me miracles,
The whole referring, yet each distinct and in its place.

To me every hour of the light and dark is a miracle,
Every cubic inch of space is a miracle,
Every square yard of the surface of the earth is spread
    with the same,
Every foot of the interior swarms with the same.

To me the sea is a continual miracle,
The fishes that swim — the rocks — the motion of the
    waves — the ships with men in them,
What stranger miracles are there?

"In wilderness I sense the miracle of life,
and behind it our scientific accomplishments fade to trivia."

~Charles Lindbergh
Life, 22 December, 1967

42

Constructing The House

Who includes diversity and is Nature,
Who is the amplitude of the earth, and the coarseness
    and sexuality of the earth, and the great charity of
    the earth, and the equilibrium also,
Who has not look'd forth from the windows the eyes
    for nothing, or whose brain held audience with
    messengers for nothing,
Who contains believers and disbelievers, who is the
    most majestic lover,
Who holds duly his or her triune proportion of realism,
    spiritualism, and of the aesthetic or intellectual,
Who having consider'd the body finds all its organs and
    parts good,
Who, out of the theory of the earth and of his or her
    body understands by subtle analogies all other
    theories,
The theory of a city, a poem, and of the large politics of
    these States;
Who believes not only in our globe with its sun and
    moon, but in other globes with their suns and
    moons,
Who, constructing the house of himself or herself,
    not for a day but for all time, sees races, eras, dates,
    generations,
The past, the future, dwelling there, like space,
    inseparable together.

"It is possible we do not yet understand
the true pathology of homesickness ...
Have wood, field, rock, and stream vested in us
something of theirs?"

~ Edith M. Thomas
The Round Year

43

Storm Music

Proud music of the storm,
Blast that careers so free, whistling across the prairies,
Strong hum of forest tree-tops—wind of the
    mountains,
Personified dim shapes—you hidden orchestras,
You serenades of phantoms with instruments alert,
Bending with Nature's rhythmus all the tongues of
    nations;
You chords left as by vast composers—you choruses,
You formless, free, religious dances—you from the
    Orient,
You undertone of rivers, roar of pouring cataracts,
You sounds from distant guns with galloping cavalry,
Echoes of camps with all the different bugle-calls,
Trooping tumultuous, filling the midnight late, bending
    me powerless,
Entering my lonesome slumber-chamber, why have
    you seiz'd me?

Come forward O my soul, and let the rest retire,
Listen, lose not, it is toward thee they tend,
Parting the midnight, entering my slumber-chamber,
For thee they sing and dance O soul.

.   .   .   .

Now the great organ sounds,
Tremulous, while underneath, (as hid footholds of the
    earth.
On which arising rest, and leaping forth depend,
All shapes of beauty, grace, and strength, all hues we
    know,

Green blades of grass and warbling birds, children that
    gambol and play, the clouds of heaven above,)
The strong base stands, and its pulsations intermits
    not,
Bathing, supporting, merging all the rest, maternity of
    all the rest,
And with it every instrument in multitudes,
The players playing, all the world's musicians,
The solemn hymns and masses rousing adoration,
All passionate heart-chants, sorrowful appeals,
The measureless sweet vocalists of ages,
And for their solvent setting earth's own diapason,
Of winds and woods and mighty ocean waves,
A new composite orchestra, binder of years and climes,
    ten-fold renewer,
As of the far-back days the poets tell, the Paradiso,
The straying hence, the separation long, but now the
    wandering done,
The journey done, the journeyman come home,
And man and art with Nature fused again.

"It is not light that is needed, but fire;
it is not the gentle shower, but thunder.
We need the storm, the whirlwind, and the earthquake."

~ Frederick Douglass
Speech, Rochester, New York, July 4, 1852

44

The True Child Of God

Ah who shall soothe these feverish children?
Who justify these restless explorations?
Who speak the secret of impassive earth?
Who bind it to us? what is this separate Nature so
    unnatural?
What is this earth to our affections? (unloving earth,
    without a throb to answer ours,
Cold earth, the place of graves.)

Yet soul be sure the first intent remains, and shall be
    carried out,
Perhaps even now the time has arrived.

After the seas are all cross'd, (as they seem already
    cross'd,)
After the great captains and engineers have
    accomplish'd their work,
After the noble inventors, after the scientists, the
    chemist, the geologist, ethnologist,
Finally shall come the poet worthy that name,
The true son of God shall come singing his songs.

Then not your deeds only O voyagers, O scientists and
    inventors, shall be justified,
All these hearts as of fretted children shall be sooth'd,
All affection shall be fully responded to, the secret shall
    be told,
All these separations and gaps shall be taken up and
    hook'd and link'd together,

The whole earth, this cold, impassive, voiceless earth,
    shall be completely justified,
Trinitas divine shall be gloriously accomplish'd and
    compacted by the true son of God, the poet,
(He shall indeed pass the straits and conquer the
    mountains,
He shall double the cape of Good Hope to some
    purpose,)
Nature and Man shall be disjoin'd and diffused no
    more,
The true son of God shall absolutely fuse them.

*"When the earth is sacred to us,
our bodies can also be sacred to us."*

~bell hooks
Sisters of the Yam

45

Hoist The Anchor

Passage to more than India!
Are thy wings plumed indeed for such far flights?
O soul, voyagest thou indeed on voyages like those?
Disportest thou on waters such as those?
Soundest below the Sanscrit and the Vedas?
Then have thy bent unleash'd.

Passage to you, your shores, ye aged fierce enigmas!
Passage to you, to mastership of you, ye strangling
    problems!
You, strew'd with the wrecks of skeletons, that, living,
    never reach'd you.

Passage to more than India!
O secret of the earth and sky!
Of you O waters of the sea! O winding creeks and
    rivers!
Of you O woods and fields! of you strong mountains of
    my land!
Of you O prairies! of you gray rocks!
O morning red! O clouds! O rain and snows!
O day and night, passage to you!

O sun and moon and all you stars!
Sirius and Jupiter!
Passage to you!

Passage, immediate passage! the blood burns in my
    veins!
Away O soul! hoist instantly the anchor!
Cut the hawsers—haul out—shake out every sail!

Have we not stood here like trees in the ground long
   enough?
Have we not grovel'd here long enough, eating and
   drinking like mere brutes?
Have we not darken'd and dazed ourselves with books
   long enough?

Sail forth—steer for the deep waters only,
Reckless O soul, exploring, I with thee, and thou with
   me,
For we are bound where mariner has not yet dared to
   go,
And we will risk the ship, ourselves and all.

O my brave soul!
O farther farther sail!
O daring joy, but safe! are they not all the seas of God?
O farther, farther, farther sail!

"The flowing river is lost in the sea;
The illumined sage is lost in the Self.
The flowing river has become the sea;
The illumined sage has become the Self."

~Mundaka Upanishad
(Part III, 2:8)

46

Interweb

A noiseless patient spider,
I mark'd where on a little promontory it stood isolated,
Mark'd how to explore the vacant vast surrounding,
It launch'd forth filament, filament, filament, out of
    itself,
Ever unreeling them, ever tirelessly speeding them.

And you O my soul where you stand,
Surrounded, detached, in measureless oceans of space,
Ceaselessly musing, venturing, throwing, seeking the
    spheres to connect them,
Till the bridge you will need be form'd, till the ductile
    anchor hold,
Till the gossamer thread you fling catch somewhere,
    O my soul.

"Now while I was tired of a world that lectured and talked and argued and did many other noisy things ... I was by no means tired of the great silent world that did things and made no fuss about doing them."

~ Anna Botsford Comstock
Trees at Leisure

47

Upon Heaven's Lake

Hark, some wild trumpeter, some strange musician,
Hovering unseen in air, vibrates capricious tunes
    to-night.

I hear thee trumpeter, listening alert I catch thy notes,
Now pouring, whirling like a tempest round me,
Now low, subdued, now in the distance lost.

Come nearer bodiless one, haply in thee resounds
Some dead composer, haply thy pensive life
Was fill'd with aspirations high, unform'd ideals,
Waves, oceans musical, chaotically surging,
That now ecstatic ghost, close to me bending,
    thy cornet echoing, pealing,
Gives out to no one's ears but mine, but freely gives
    to mine,
That I may thee translate.

Blow trumpeter free and clear, I follow thee,
While at thy liquid prelude, glad, serene,
The fretting world, the streets, the noisy hours of day
    withdraw,

A holy calm descends like dew upon me,
I walk in cool refreshing night the walks of Paradise,
I scent the grass, the moist air and the roses;
Thy song expands my numb'd imbonded spirit, thou
    freest, launchest me,
Floating and basking upon heaven's lake.

"Joy is drunk by every creature
from Nature's breast."

~ Friedrich von Schiller
"Ode to Joy"

48

Wild Spirit

Spirit that form'd this scene,
These tumbled rock-piles grim and red,
These reckless heaven-ambitious peaks,
These gorges, turbulent-clear streams, this naked
    freshness,
These formless wild arrays, for reasons of their own,
I know thee, savage spirit—we have communed
    together,
Mine too such wild arrays, for reasons of their own;
Was't charged against my chants they had forgotten
    art?
To fuse within themselves its rules precise and
    delicatesse?
The lyrist's measur'd beat, the wrought-out temple's
    grace—column and polish'd arch forgot?
But thou that revelest here—spirit that form'd this
    scene,
They have remember'd thee.

"The one who has broken the barriers of words
has conquered limitations:
Allah or Jesus, Moses or Kali,
the rich or the poor, sage or fool,
all are one and the same to that one."

~ Song of a Baul of Bengal
The Mirror of the Sky

49

Wonderful To Be Here!

Splendor of ended day floating and filling me,
Hour prophetic, hour resuming the past,
Inflating my throat, you divine average,
You earth and life till the last ray gleams I sing.

Open mouth of my soul uttering gladness,
Eyes of my soul seeing perfection,
Natural life of me faithfully praising things,
Corroborating forever the triumph of things.

Illustrious every one!
Illustrious what we name space, sphere of unnumber'd
    spirits,
Illustrious the mystery of motion in all beings, even the
    tiniest insect,
Illustrious the attribute of speech, the senses, the body,
Illustrious the passing light—illustrious the pale
    reflection on the new moon in the western sky,
Illustrious whatever I see or hear or touch, to the last.

Good in all,
In the satisfaction and aplomb of animals,
In the annual return of the seasons,
In the hilarity of youth,
In the strength and flush of manhood,
In the grandeur and exquisiteness of old age,
In the superb vistas of death.

Wonderful to depart!
Wonderful to be here!
The heart, to jet the all-alike and innocent blood!
To breathe the air, how delicious!
To speak—to walk—to seize something by the hand!
To prepare for sleep, for bed, to look on my rose-color'd
    flesh!
To be conscious of my body, so satisfied, so large!
To be this incredible God I am!
To have gone forth among other Gods, these men and
    women I love.

Wonderful how I celebrate you and myself!

"Above all, it is not necessary that we should have
any unexpected, extraordinary experiences in meditation."

~ Dietrich Bonhoeffer
Life Together

50

My Windows My Eyes

O amazement of things—even the least particle!
O spirituality of things!
O strain musical flowing through ages and continents,
    now reaching me and America!
I take your strong chords, intersperse them, and
    cheerfully pass them forward.
I too carol the sun, usher'd or at noon, or as now,
    setting,
I too throb to the brain and beauty of the earth and of
    all the growths of the earth,
I too have felt the resistless call of myself.

As I steam'd down the Mississippi,
As I wander'd over the prairies,
As I have lived, as I have look'd through my windows
    my eyes,
As I went forth in the morning, as I beheld the light
    breaking in the east,
As I bathed on the beach of the Eastern Sea, and again
    on the beach of the Western Sea,
As I roam'd the streets of inland Chicago, whatever
    streets I have roam'd,
Or cities or silent woods, or even amid the sights of
    war,
Wherever I have been I have charged myself with
    contentment and triumph.

I sing to the last the equalities modern or old,
I sing the endless finales of things,
I say Nature continues, glory continues,
I praise with electric voice,
For I do not see one imperfection in the universe,
And I do not see one cause or result lamentable at last
   in the universe.

O setting sun! though the time has come,
I still warble under you, if none else does,
   unmitigated adoration.

"Something of the miracle of Nature is revealed to me ...
To me a lush carpet of pine needles or spongy grass
is more welcome than the most luxurious Persian rug.
At times my heart cries out with longing to see all these things.
If I can get so much pleasure from mere touch,
how much more beauty must be revealed by sight.
Yet, those who have eyes apparently see little."

~ Helen Keller
Three Days to See

51

Tents Of Green

Lo, the camps of the tents of green,
Which the days of peace keep filling, and the days of
   war keep filling,
With a mystic army, (is it too order'd forward? is it too
   only halting awhile,
Till night and sleep pass over?)
Now in those camps of green, in their tents dotting the
   world,
In the parents, children, husbands, wives, in them, in
   the old and young,
Sleeping under the sunlight, sleeping under the
   moonlight, content and silent there at last,
Behold the mighty bivouac-field and waiting-camp of
   all,
Of the corps and generals all, and the President over
   the corps and generals all,
And of each of us O soldiers, and of each and all in the
   ranks we fought,
(There without hatred we all, all meet.)

For presently O soldiers, we too camp in our place in
   the bivouac-camps of green,
But we need not provide for outposts, nor word for the
   counter-sign,
Nor drummer to beat the morning drum.

"Those who keep their duty to their Creator
are drven into the Garden in troops till … the gates are opened,
and the keepers say to them: Peace be unto you!"

~ Qur'an
(Surah 39:73)

52

Of Joy, Sweet Joy

As they draw to a close,
Of what underlies the precedent songs—of my aims
    in them,
Of the seed I have sought to plant in them,
Of joy, sweet joy, through many a year, in them,
(For them, for them have I lived, in them my work is
    done,)
Of many an aspiration fond, of many a dream and
    plan;
Through Space and Time fused in a chant, and the
    flowing eternal identity,
To Nature encompassing these, encompassing God—
    to the joyous, electric all,
To the sense of Death, and accepting exulting in Death
    in its turn the same as life,
The entrance of man to sing;
To compact you, ye parted, diverse lives,
To put rapport the mountains and rocks and streams,
And the winds of the north, and the forests of oak
    and pine,
With you O soul.

"In this hour divinely fresh and still, the fair face of every flower salutes me with a silent joy that fills me with infinite content."

~ Celia Laighton Thaxter
An Island Garden

53

Let Go The Ropes

Now final   to the shore,
Now land and life final   and farewell,
Now Voyager depart, (much, much for thee is yet
   in store,)
Often enough hast thou adventur'd o'er the seas,
Cautiously cruising, studying the charts,
Duly again to port and hawser's tie returning,
But now obey thy cherish'd secret wish,
Embrace thy friends, leave all in order,
To port and hawser's tie no more returning,
Depart upon thy endless cruise old Sailor.

"Like swans leaving a lake, the thoughtful abandon one attachment after another."

~ Gautama Buddha
Dhammapada (7:2)

54

Nothing Can Be Lost

Nothing is ever really lost, or can be lost,
No birth, identity, form—no object of the world,
Nor life, nor force, nor any visible thing;
Appearance must not foil, nor shifted sphere confuse
    thy brain.
Ample are time and space—ample the fields of Nature.
The body, sluggish, aged, cold—the embers left from
    earlier fires,
The light in the eye grown dim, shall duly flame again;
The sun now low in the west rises for mornings and for
    noons continual;
To frozen clods ever the spring's invisible law returns,
With grass and flowers and summer fruits and corn.

"O landscape of my birth
you have never been far from my heart.
It is I who have been far.
If you will take me back
Know that I
Am yours."

~ Alice Walker
"My Heart Has Reopened to You: The Place Where I Was Born"

55

Rain

And who art thou? said I to the soft-falling shower,
Which, strange to tell, gave me an answer, as here
   translated:
I am the Poem of Earth, said the voice of the rain,
Eternal I rise impalpable out of the land and the
   bottomless sea,
Upward to heaven, whence, vaguely form'd, altogether
   changed, and yet the same,
I descend to lave the drouths, atomies, dust-layers of
   the globe,
And all that in them without me were seeds only,
   latent, unborn;
And forever, by day and night, I give back life to my
   own origin and make pure and beautify it;
(For song, issuing from its birth-place, after fulfilment,
   wandering,
Reck'd or unreck'd, duly with love returns.)

*"May my teaching drop as the rain, my speech distil as the dew,
as the gentle rain upon the tender grass,
and as the showers upon the herb."*

~ Torah
Deuteronomy 32

56

Simple Shows

Soon shall the winter's foil be here;
Soon shall these icy ligatures unbind and melt—A little
   while,
And air, soil, wave, suffused shall be in softness, bloom
   and growth—a thousand forms shall rise
From these dead clods and chills as from low burial
   graves.
Thine eyes, ears—all thy best attributes—all that takes
   cognizance of natural beauty,
Shall wake and fill.
Thou shalt perceive the simple shows, the delicate
   miracles of earth,
Dandelions, clover, the emerald grass, the early scents
   and flowers,
The arbutus under foot, the willow's yellow-green, the
   blossoming plum and cherry;
With these the robin, lark and thrush, singing their
   songs—the flitting bluebird;
For such the scenes the annual play brings on.

*"Find joy in the sky, in the trees, in the flowers.
There are flowers everywhere
for those who want to see them."*

~ Henri Matisse
Jazz

57

Sunset

Shot gold, maroon and violet, dazzling silver, emerald,
    fawn,
The earth's whole amplitude and Nature's multiform
    power consign'd for once to colors;
The light, the general air possess'd by them—colors till
    now unknown,
No limit, confine—not the Western sky alone—the
    high meridian—North, South, all,
Pure luminous color fighting the silent shadows to
    the last.

"She remembered the real grass that moved and changed
like a sea of silk. It took one color from the north,
other colors from the south and the east and the west...
There was great power and love in the earth then."

~ Meridel Le Sueur
The Ancient People and the Newly Come

58

Touch Of Flame

The touch of flame—the illuminating fire—the loftiest
  look at last,
O'er city, passion, sea—o'er prairie, mountain, wood—
  the earth itself;
The airy, different, changing hues of all, in falling
  twilight,
Objects and groups, bearings, faces, reminiscences;
The calmer sight—the golden setting, clear and broad:
So much i' the atmosphere, the points of view,
  the situations whence we scan,
Bro't out by them alone—so much (perhaps the best)
  unreck'd before;
The lights indeed from them—old age's lambent peaks.

"The whole world is charged with the glory of God
and I feel fire and music under my feet."

~ Thomas Merton
Sign of Jonas

59

I Feel The Sky

Ah, whispering, something again, unseen,
Where late this heated day thou enterest at my
  window, door,
Thou, laving, tempering all, cool-freshing, gently
  vitalizing
Me, old, alone, sick, weak-down, melted-worn with
  sweat;
Thou, nestling, folding close and firm yet soft,
  companion better than talk, book, art;
(Thou hast, O Nature! elements! utterance to my heart
  beyond the rest—and this is of them,)
So sweet thy primitive taste to breathe within—
  thy soothing fingers on my face and hands,
Thou, messenger-magical strange bringer to body and
  spirit of me,
(Distances balk'd—occult medicines penetrating me
  from head to foot,)
I feel the sky, the prairie vast—I feel the mighty
  northern lakes,
I feel the ocean and the forest—somehow I feel the
  globe itself swift-swimming in space;
Thou blown from lips so loved, now gone—
  haply from endless store, God-sent,
(For thou art spiritual, Godly, most of all known to
  my sense,)

Minister to speak to me, here and now, what word has
    never told, and cannot tell,
Art thou not universal concrete's distillation?
Law's, all Astronomy's last refinement?
Hast thou no soul?
Can I not know, identify thee?

"National boundaries are not evidenced when we view the earth
from space. Fanatic ethnic or religious or national identifications
are a little difficult to support when we see our planet as a fragile,
blue crescent fading to become an inconspicuous point of light
against the bastion and citadel of the stars."

~Carl Sagan
Cosmos

60

Strangely Hidden

For his o'erarching and last lesson the greybeard sufi,
In the fresh scent of the morning in the open air,
On the slope of a teeming Persian rose-garden,
Under an ancient chestnut-tree wide spreading its
    branches,
Spoke to the young priests and students.

"Finally my children, to envelop each word, each part
    of the rest,
Allah is all, all, all—is immanent in every life and
    object,
May-be at many and many-a-more removes—
    yet Allah, Allah, Allah is there.

"Has the estray wander'd far?
Is the reason-why strangely hidden?
Would you sound below the restless ocean of the
    entire world?
Would you know the dissatisfaction? the urge and
    spur of every life;
The something never still'd—never entirely gone? the
    invisible need of every seed?

"It is the central urge in every atom,
  (Often unconscious, often evil, downfallen,)
To return to its divine source and origin, however
    distant,
Latent the same in subject and in object, without one
    exception."

"I want to grow throughout my life, Like a blossoming tree,
Taking my nourishment from dirt,
And spreading my arms to the heavens
in all seasons."

~ Suzanne Walker
Rainbow Round the Moon

Afterword

You Shall Be A Great Poem

This is what you shall do: Love the earth and sun and the animals, despise riches, give alms to every one that asks, stand up for the stupid and crazy, devote your income and labor to others, hate tyrants, argue not concerning God, have patience and indulgence toward the people, take off your hat to nothing known or unknown or to any one or number of persons, go freely with powerful uneducated persons and with the young and with the mothers of families, read these leaves in the open air every season of every year of your life, re-examine all you have been told at school or church or in any book, dismiss whatever insults your own soul, and your very flesh shall be a great poem and have the richest fluency not only in its words but in the silent lines of its lips and face and between the lashes of your eyes and in every motion and joint of your body.... The poet shall not spend time in unneeded work. He shall know that the ground is always ready plowed and manured.... He shall go directly to the creation.

from "Preface" (Leaves of Grass, 1855 edition)

Sources

In the preceding text the source of each Whitman selection is identified by a particular leaf icon, shown following the passage. Below is a key to those sources:

Song Of The Open Road

Calamus:
   Earth, My Likeness (selection 2)
   Roots And Leaves Themselves Alone
     (selection 5)

Children of Adam:
   To The Garden The World (selection 3)
   We Two, How Long We Were Fool'd
     (selection 4)

Song Of Myself

Salut Au Monde!

Crossing Brooklyn Ferry

143

Source Texts:

Complete Poetry and Selected Prose by Walt Whitman. Edited by James E. Miller. Boston: Houghton Mifflin Company, 1959 (in the public domain, except for the introduction).

Walt Whitman. Leaves of Grass. New York: New American Library (Penguin), 1958 (in the public domain, except for the introduction).

Other sources consulted:

Roy Morris, Jr. The Better Angel: Walt Whitman in the Civil War. New York: Oxford University Press, 2000.

Robert D. Richardson, Jr. Emerson: The Mind On Fire. University of California Press, 1995.

Meditations of Walt Whitman: Earth, My Likeness was created on a Power Macintosh G3, using QuarkXPress 4.1 and Adobe Photoshop 5.5. The text and display font is Bitstream's *Calligraphic 810*; the "leaf" icons belong to Andrew D. Taylor's *ArborisFolium*; and the "book" and "grain stalk" graphics belong to P22's *Arts and Crafts Ornaments 2* and *Da Vinci*, respectively.

Photo Credits

*C*hris Highland is an interspiritual chaplain, author, songwriter and poet. He completed his under- graduate studies in religion and philosophy in Seattle, Washington before settling in the San Francisco Bay Area to complete his Masters degree. A passionate saunterer, he enjoys an intimate rela- tion with Nature in forests, mountains and water- falls. An avowed heretic ("one who seeks new paths"), Chris' writing reflects his exploration of the edges of human society and his playful search for what Emerson called "high, clear and spiritual con- versation," to be had by each and every one of us as "beggars on the highway."

Chris is the author of *Meditations of John Muir: Nature's Temple*, *Meditations of Henry David Thoreau: A Light in the Woods*, and *Meditations of Ralph Waldo Emerson: Into the Green Future*, all from Wilderness Press. An eclectic map of Chris' creative thought and colorful photog- raphy can be read and seen at www.naturetemple.net.

More meditations...

Meditations of
John Muir:
Nature's Temple

Insightful quotations from America's preeminent naturalist, writer, and activist are paired with selections from other celebrated thinkers and spiritual texts.

ISBN 0-89997-285-3

Meditations of
Henry David Thoreau:
A Light in the Woods

A sampler of 60 thoughtful quotations from America's first great conservationist and incomparable social critic, paired with reflections from other spiritual traditions.

ISBN 0-89997-321-3

Meditations of
Ralph Waldo Emerson:
Into the Green Future

Selections from 30 years of Emerson's writings reveal the essence of this great author, poet and philosopher, along with quotations from historical and contemporary thinkers.

ISBN 0-89997-352-3

Printed in the USA
CPSIA information can be obtained
at www.ICGtesting.com
JSHW011522130424
61126JS00005B/18